Lisa
You're
Unstoppable
No limits.
Love Ya
Meeda Pulley

signed on
Friday June 4th, 2010

You're
Just
unstoppable
No limits
any
Opportunity

UNSTOPPABLE FAITH
Discovering the Indestructible You
Orrin K. Pullings, Sr.

Published By:
The "LIGHT" Designs Book Publishers
A division of Kingdom Publishing Group, Inc.
P.O. Box 505, Ashland, VA 23005
www.kingdompublishing.org

©2008 by Orrin K. Pullings, Sr.
Library of Congress

ISBN: 978-0-9801564-5-4

Cover Design by: Matthew Williams, Sr.

All rights reserved. No part of this book, including contents and/or cover, may be reproduced in whole or in part in any form without the expressed written consent of the author and/or publisher.

Printed in the United States of America.

DEDICATION

This book is dedicated to:

My wife, my love and the queen of my heart. My best friend. I want to thank you for your commitment and dedication to my success. You are my inspiration. I love you honey. The best is yet to come!

My children Orrin Jr., Elijah, James, Zacchaeus, and my daughter, baby Medina and my God-daughter, Nannie. Thank you for your support. Daddy loves you.

My mom and dad James and Esther Pullings, pastors of Leviticus Church of God in Christ (Queens, NY). Thank you for the faith that I inherited from you guys. You are an awesome example for my life. I love you.

My spiritual sons and daughters, members, and partners of United Nations Church International of Richmond, VA, New York, Georgia and South Carolina. You guys are the best.

To those who helped make this book possible: Yolanda, Sheena, Milondra and Nina. Thank you. You were a big help and a big inspiration to this whole process.

I acknowledge my Lord and Savior, Jesus Christ, as the Head of my life.

Without Him, none of this could be possible.

TABLE OF CONTENTS

Introduction 9

Faith That Yields God's Glory 17

Understanding Faith 23

Dimensions of Faith 37

Perception 57

From Promise to Possession 69

The Predestined You 105

The Unstoppable You 111

The Indestructible You 119

INTRODUCTION

We often make predictions about our future based on what *is* rather than what is to be. We limit ourselves and our faith to what we can see, instead of the promises of God. As believers in Jesus Christ, we must start making decisions and planning our future based on His Word and the plans He has for us--plans of good and not evil.

"...For I know the plans I have for you, declares the Lord, plans to prosper you, plans to give you hope and a future."
Jeremiah 29:11 (NIV)

Knowing God's word and having the steadfast, immovable faith to believe that what He promised is true will enable you to look past your current circumstances and start building your life around what God has in mind for you.

As you read this book you may be experiencing trials, but that is only because God is trying to achieve glory in your life. With each trial you are being strengthened, purified and glorified. Glory does not just happen. You grow in glory. You grow from glory to glory to glory. Each time, God is trying to achieve another dimension of glory in you and out of you. Such glorification does not happen instantly. It is a process.

It is just like when I go to get my jewelry polished; it has to go through a process before it can shine properly. My jeweler takes my ring and places it against a polishing block. When he takes it from the block it looks worse than it did before he started. The next thing he does is dip the ring into a solution and spins it around a buffing/polishing machine. When he takes it off, my ring is shining much more than it was before I gave it to him.

Just like with my jewelry, you too may experience times when you do not appear to be blessed. You may even feel that you are in a whirlwind of problems from which you will never recover and that the promises of God are not true. Do not believe these deceptions. You must take your position based on the word of God.

> *"Casting down imaginations, and every
> high thing that exalteth itself against
> the knowledge of God, and bringing
> into captivity every thought to
> the obedience of Christ..."*
> *II Corinthians 10:5 (KJV)*

Do not be afraid or allow people to put you down because things do not look so bright right now. You are in the polishing process.

Before God can bring out the radiance and real shine of the King or Queen you are, sometimes He has to dull you first. He has to put you in dull situations that make you look messed up and appear like nothing good is going to come out of you. Remember, God is perfecting you and taking you to another dimension of glory. In 1 Peter 5:8-9 (AMP) we are commanded to:

> *"Be well balanced (temperate, sober of mind),
> be vigilant and cautious at all times;
> for that enemy of yours, the devil, roams
> around like a lion roaring [in fierce hunger],
> seeking someone to seize upon and devour.*

Withstand him; be firm in faith [against his onset--rooted, established, strong, immovable, and determined], knowing that the same (identical) sufferings are appointed to your brotherhood (the whole body of Christians) throughout the world."

The word "resist" means to fight against or to contend with. It means that you are not supposed to run from the enemy. James 4:7 (KJV) says,

"Submit yourselves therefore to God. Resist the devil and he will flee from you."

You cannot let the enemy take over your life. You have to get in your war position.

"Put on the whole armour of God, that ye may be able to stand against the wiles of the devil."
Ephesians 6:11 (KJV)

Although it may appear that he is winning right now, you have more power than he does. He may be affecting your finances, but fight against what he is trying to do. If he is coming against your business, resist the enemy by investing more. Keep the resistance up. Expand. Enlarge. Increase. Find any way you can to resist him. He might have whipped you yesterday, but don't lose the fight in you. Never let your trials take away your fight.

Any good fighter has to have a good corner man. After you have been beat up in the first round, you need someone in your corner to tell you that it is going to be all right. You need someone to put some water on your face and grease you up. You need someone to tell you about your good qualities. You need a corner man to say, "You are doing good man, keep up the good work and go out there and keep on fighting." We all need someone, from time to time, who will tell us that we can win! Praise God I have that in my wife, Medina, an excellent spiritual motivator.

And that's what I want to be for you, my friend, through this book...a spiritual motivator, a 'corner man'. I want to remind you, as it is stated in 1 Peter 4:12-14 (AMP), that you should not be surprised at the painful trial you are suffering, as though something strange were happening to you. Rather, you should rejoice that you participate in the sufferings of Christ, so that you may be overjoyed when His glory is revealed. If you are insulted because of the name of Christ, you are blessed, for the Spirit of glory and of God rests on you. I want you to know that if you are a partaker of Christ's suffering—of His pain—and if you can endure like Christ endured, the spirit of glory shall rest upon you. That means the same glory that is on Jesus Christ right now; the same power that resurrected Him from the dead on the third day is going to be the same resurrection power that is going to raise you up. The same power will raise you from the ghetto to your mansion. The same power will raise you from welfare into millions. The glory of the Lord will raise you up and nobody can stop or hinder it, but you.

Do not be blinded by your status. Do not let what you look like today hold you back because your current status cannot define who you really are. Who you really are is who God says you are and who He has designed for you to be. Sometimes, however, you can only access that picture of yourself by faith.

As you read this book, I pray that your faith will grow to the point of being unstoppable, for there is nothing that you cannot achieve at that level. It shares what you need to know and do to attain unstoppable faith. I believe that if you meditate on and institute these principles, unstoppable faith can be yours.

So, get ready to discover all that you need so that nothing can stop you! Get ready to possess your unstoppable faith!

Faith that Yields God's Glory

FAITH THAT YIELDS GOD'S GLORY

What is the "Glory" of God?

The Glory of God is God Himself showing forth, revealing, and manifesting the magnificence of His character to His creation. God is infinite. He is omniscient (all-knowing), omnipotent (all-powerful) and omnipresent (everywhere at the same time). When His glory shines forth in our lives, we become eligible partakers and distributors of His wisdom, His power and His presence.

The Promise of God's Glory

God assures us that He is with us as we surrender our desires, our intellect and our agendas to Him.

> *"Draw near to God and*
> *he will come near to you..."*
> *James 4:8 (NKJV)*

When we become less people-focused and more God-centered, He responds by widely opening up the windows of heaven and pouring out His spirit (His very presence) upon us. To experience God's glory we must die to self, daily (to continually empty ourselves of our fleshly needs) so that God can enter in, take up residence, and operate fully on our behalf. This process is not always easy but the reward is well worth it. The Apostle Paul states it clearly:

> *"For I consider that the sufferings of this present time (this present life) are not worth being compared with the glory that is about to be revealed to us and in us and for us and conferred on us!"*
> *Romans 8:18 (AMP)*

Experiencing God's Glory

Often times, when people experience trials they view them as a sign of personal failure or overall disobedience to God. They feel that it is their punishment for something they must have done to bring such turmoil into their lives. This trick has caused many of God's people to lose their faith and hope of ever experiencing God's divine presence. The truth is, when we experience difficult times, and we draw nearer to God, it is an opportunity for God to move mightily and reveal His glory not only in us but also to the world.

"For [even the whole] creation (all nature) waits expectantly and longs earnestly for God's sons to be made known [waits for the revealing, the disclosing of their sonship]."
Romans 8:19 (AMP)

When God's presence manifests, changes come. People, circumstances and environments are transformed at the very presence of God's glory. When we walk in God's glory our spiritual fruit will be plentiful; we will have a glorified presence just like Jesus and a ministry that is filled with the Holy Spirit with signs and wonders following all to which we set our hands. Our light—the light of Christ—will shine so brightly that the world will not be able to deny the power of God's presence.

How timely it is for the world to see God's glory revealed in the body of Christ. In the midst of all the negative publicity that the church has received of late, we need a revival. To experience

God's true presence in our lives, and to have it revealed through us to others, is both empowering and motivating to the body of Christ and to the world. It will be a powerful testament to all of who God is, as they see His presence manifested in, and experienced by, the believers.

Growing in Faith from Glory to Glory

The foundational substance that is needed to catapult us from glory to glory, and that is essential to our partaking of the manifest presence of God, is Faith. Through each hope, through each trial, through each anticipation, our faith must be present and in full effect… steadfast and immovable… nothing wavering.

This may seem like a tall order for us, especially during those times when we are not able to see "The Light" in the midst of our darkness. However, it is our faith that keeps us moving. We may be weak in faith when we start out, but each time God manifests His presence (His glory) in our lives, in spite of our "little faith," He strengthens us and causes our faith to grow.

And, as our faith grows, our Godly foundation is fortified and our endurance is built up thus enabling us to stand.

It is essential that we perpetually develop and increase our Faith. As we do this, our expectation of receiving more of God is broadened, enabling us to continuously grow in faith and from glory to glory.

Understanding Faith

UNDERSTANDING FAITH

Faith Defined

Before we go any further, we must establish the definition and understanding of faith that will guide us in this book. Faith is the evidence (the convincing proof) or demonstration of what you cannot see. Faith reveals the truth based on the word of God. Therefore, faith is the reality of what we hope for. It is the conviction of what God has foreordained and predestined in our lives.

"NOW FAITH is the assurance (the confirmation, the title deed) of the things [we] hope for, being the proof of things [we] do not see and the conviction of their reality [faith perceiving as real fact what is not revealed to the senses]."
Hebrews 11:1 (AMP)

Even though I do not see it, I am convinced that it exists.

Just like some of the other planets that exist in our solar system, we cannot see them with our natural eye… Jupiter, Mars, etc., but it still does not take away from their reality. They are there.

There are also things about you that you cannot see now, but they are there. God placed them in you before you were even born. They have not manifested yet but the seed of it exists in you.

In Genesis 1:1, when God created the heavens and the earth, the earth was without form and void. But if you read verse 12, God told the earth to bring forth the seed that was in itself:

"And the earth brought forth grass, and herb yielding seed after his kind, and the tree yielding fruit, whose seed was in itself, after his kind: and God saw that it was good."
Genesis 1:12 (KJV)

So the Lord did not have to say, "tree here," "flower here," "rose bush there," God said, "Earth bring forth!" and the earth produced its predestined, horticultural purpose. In verse 1, it was without form and void, but after God made its environment conducive, such as separating daytime from night and separating dry grounds from the waters, it was now time for the earth to do its part—bring forth what was already placed inside it.

After God gets finished creating your environment—eliminating some people from your life, adding some people to your life, putting you in the right places, and taking you from the wrong places—you are going to hear a voice from God telling you to "bring forth" what is inside of you. It is time to start being convicted about the reality of your future existence. Start letting your faith not just be a saying, but a conviction as well.

Have you ever felt convicted about doing wrong? Does it grieve you and keep you up all night confessing, "Oh Lord I am sorry?" Whenever you are convicted, a weight sits on your heart. You ought to be as confident in God as you are convicted about your wrongdoing. With the same strength that you cry out, "I am sorry," to God, you ought to cry out, "I know God is going to do it!" "I know in whom I believe!"

NOW FAITH

Your unstoppable faith is a NOW FAITH. As you walk with the Lord and get to know Him better, you will enter into seasons of your life where you need God to do some things immediately. At those times, you will need NOW FAITH!

Hebrews 11:1 (AMP) says, "Now faith is the assurance, confirmation, or the title deed of things we hoped for, proof of things we do not see, the conviction (or the state of being convinced) of things not seen." In other words, faith is your ability to not see a thing in the natural, but to be fully convinced that what God said already exists. You may not be able to see, trace, feel, or even sense that for which you have been hoping, yet you still believe it will happen. When you walk in NOW FAITH, you do not throw in the towel, compromise, or settle because you are convinced that what you are hoping and believing God for, you will receive.

There are several things you need to know about NOW FAITH. The first thing you need to know has to do with the concept of confirmation. When you apply faith to your life, you have the confirmation. There are many times that I travel on planes without physically having a ticket.

However, before I get to the airport, I am given a confirmation number. With that number, I know that my seat cannot be sold. My seat is guaranteed. The only thing I have to do is arrive on time. It works this way with faith too. You have the confirmation; you just need to get there on time. For example, those of you who are seeking a mate need to be in the right place at the right time because God already has Mr. or Ms. Right lined up for you. Do not get caught up with a quick fix or someone the devil sends because that will surely delay you. The tricks of the enemy will delay you. Move in the timing of God. Confirmations are only available for a certain period.

In addition to confirmation, faith also gives you the title deed or proof of ownership. For example, someone may borrow your vehicle, but he or she cannot claim it as his or her own because the title deed has your name on it. They can go wherever they want, but it is still your car. In the same manner, that which God has for you has your name on it. No matter who has it, they must release it when your time comes because it is yours.

Faith literally sets up your tomorrow today. Faith starts NOW. When it hits your life, it confirms what will happen tomorrow. Romans 4:17 (KJV) says, "As it is written, I have made thee a father of many nations..." God was telling Abraham who he was going to become. The Bible reveals this again in Jeremiah chapter one. God told Jeremiah that in his tomorrow he would be a prophet to the nations. Jeremiah was only a child when he received this word and struggled to receive it. Jeremiah's response to God was, "Lord, I cannot speak for I am only a child." And the Lord said, "Do not say you are a child." Jeremiah gets rebuked for speaking his today and his reality. The Lord says, "Don't say it." So, if Jeremiah was not allowed to say what he was currently, that meant he was supposed to speak His future existence. Jeremiah said, "child;" God said, "prophet," simply because he was predestined to be a prophet unto the nations. You need to start speaking your destiny rather than your today's reality.

Sometimes we focus so much on where we are now that we cannot celebrate the word for our tomorrow. But when you have a word from God about your tomorrow, you should get excited about it. If you are struggling with unbelief in relation to the word that God has given you, know that whenever there is a call or God is taking you somewhere, He always sends confirmation. Jesus Christ himself was confirmed and received affirmation. When John baptized Jesus in the Jordan River, the Father looked down on Jesus—who at that point had not worked one miracle—and said, "This is my beloved son in whom I am well pleased." Although the ministry of Jesus had just begun, the Father confirmed and affirmed Him.

When you have confirmation on your destiny, you need affirmation. This is why it is vital for you to receive mentoring and training from someone who will affirm your purpose. Sometimes your mom or dad cannot affirm it, but you need to be around someone who will. Confirmation needs affirmation. You have to make faith statements. When you make faith statements of things that do not exist in your life right now, it brings affirmation to the confirmation.

You have to get bold enough to start speaking things that are not. God will not make you embarrassed or ashamed. You have to have enough faith to start declaring it:

*It is not, but I declare it is.
It has not happened yet, but I decree
and declare that it is and it shall come to pass.*

You have to do this even when everything seems to be working against your manifestation or promise. Faith is going to be your transportation. It will be faith that takes you from now to the place of manifestation. You are going to need faith to carry you through all the dilemmas which you will face. The enemy wants to make you think that you are going to be stuck, but you are just walking through the valley. You are getting ready to come out with the victory. You are getting ready to come out with more than you had before you started. It is time for you to start believing and speaking those things which do not exist as if they did exist. You must understand the power of the Holy Spirit as your down payment on every promise that God has ever made to you. As it says in Ephesians 1:14, the Holy Spirit is the guarantee of your inheritance (the first fruit, the pledge, and foretaste, the down payment on our heritage). He authenticates the value of the glory that is getting ready to come into our lives. You need to affirm this in your spirit right now:

Thank You Jesus for Your Holy Spirit, because Your spirit is just the down payment on everything else that You promised me. Hallelujah!!!

In the book of Hebrews 12:2 (KJV), the Bible says, "Looking unto Jesus the author and finisher of our faith…" He is the writer and designer of our faith. He is the author and finisher. God is a good writer and creates good scripts. I believe that if we would start looking at the script and find out what the end says, our faith would not waver. God is the author and the finisher, the master planner. He has a way of making scenes very exciting and dramatic.

Have you had some challenging or exciting things to happen to you lately? If so, you are in good company. Consider Job. One day as Job (Chapters 1&2) was in his house, some messengers came to him with devastating news. The first message sounded something like this: "Job, you have lost all your livestock. They came and raided you and took everything. Job, you are finished." After that messenger, another one says, "Listen Job, you have lost everything, including your children." Talk about exciting and dramatic.

Every time I read the book of Job it is intriguing to see how much patience He possessed. However, we see that as Job is consistent with God, things start to change. That is the key. We must learn to be consistent in bad predicaments. What I mean by consistency is being constant in personality, in emotions and in praise. I am going to consistently praise God in spite of everything that I am facing. I am not going to let my dilemmas change the praiser that I am. I am not going to let my circumstances change the worshipper that I am. If you live a lifestyle of authentic praise and worship, circumstances cannot change you. The enemy leaves Job's wife alive and Job's consistency does not make sense to her. Your consistency does not have to make sense to everybody. Your tithing and giving offerings while you still have financial problems may not make sense to those around you. But you being constant is because of your personal relationship with God. Job's wife's response was like, "Job, you are crazy. Why do you hold on? Curse God and die." Job held on to his confession saying, "He knows the way that I take." That means the designer knows the path. He knows what I am facing tomorrow. He will not put more on me than I am able to bear. He knows the way that I take and when He has tried me I shall come forth as gold. God knows the way you are going and He is taking you this way because He is designing something great at the end. So great tribulation now, brings greater manifestation later.

Whenever there is a construction site, things are in disarray at first. It is the same way with our lives. Things begin out of order, but you have to know that God is building something. Because He is the designer and author of our faith, He knows the beginning and He also knows the end. We have to use our imaginations and start turning the chapters of our lives.

You will find a major difference between chapters 1 and 2 and chapter 42 of the book of Job. In chapter 42, God reverses the captivity of Job. God turns everything around and gives him double. The only thing you have to do is turn the page and realize that your tomorrow is going to be better than your today. If there is trouble in your life, know that it is all a part of the script. If you are crying today, the Writer plans for you to rejoice tomorrow. God is a great author. Dramatic tribulation brings dramatic victory. If you can make it through chapters 1 and 2, through to chapter 42, you will find out that everything is going to get better for you. You will find that all that you have dealt with was worth it.

Looking unto Jesus who is the author and finisher of our faith… Hebrews 12:3 (KJV) says, "Consider Him that endured such contradiction of sinners..." Whenever you start believing God you better expect contradictions. That means there are some things that will go contrary to what you believe God for, but if you can endure the contradiction, then your days of celebration are on the way, because you have been destined for *greatness*.

You can confirm, confess and profess your future right now because God is not subject to this time only. He is Omnipresent. He is every place at the same time and in all time zones. All you have to do is walk upright, live for God, and you will start bumping into stuff. What made Abraham stronger in faith was that he knew how to believe the things that God had promised. He knew he had the confirmation and the title deed. You already possess what God promised. It is already yours. It is time to start speaking and living your future. The minute you declare and believe it, it begins to exist.

Dimensions of Faith

DIMENSIONS OF FAITH

*Dimension: a level of existence
or consciousness.*
(Merriam-Webster Dictionary)

Once you understand what faith is, then you need to know that there are various aspects of faith. Four dimensions of faith that I believe you must experience before you can transition to unstoppable faith are: a measure of faith, inherited faith, proactive faith, and faith knowing.

A Measure of Faith

Measure: an adequate or due portion.
(Merriam-Webster Dictionary)

According to the book of Romans 12:3, God has distributed to each man a measure of faith. From the moment you believed and trusted God, there was a measure of faith that was inherent from God. This faith gives you enough confidence to believe that Jesus died for our sins and rose again on the third day. This faith enables you to believe in a God that you cannot see, feel or touch.

Inherited Faith

Inherit: to receive by the transmission of hereditary factors.
(Dictionary.com)

In addition to the measure of faith that God gives us, we can also inherit faith from our family members, people we have read about in the Bible, or other believers through whom we have seen God demonstrate His power.

One Biblical example of someone inheriting faith can be found in II Timothy 1:5 (NIV). There, the apostle Paul says to Timothy, "I have been reminded of your sincere faith which first lived in your grandmother Lois and in your mother Eunice and, I am persuaded, now lives in you also." The apostle Paul saw in Timothy the same faith that he had seen in Timothy's grandmother and mother. Timothy had inherited faith.

It is good to know that the faith and ensuing confidence that God has released in my life is not just for me. It is good to know that my children can see my confidence in Jesus Christ and inherit it. Starting today, we must live a life of faith before our children so that they can inherit and walk in that faith.

In some regards, inherited faith is a dimension of faith that you receive passively. In other words, you do not have to do anything other than just be and live to receive it. For example, a child does not have to do anything other than be born to inherit features from his mom or dad. One just receives a measure of his/her parent's features or characteristics by being born to them.

As I grew up, I witnessed my dad, who is a pastor, go through a lot of things in his ministry and in his personal life. Every time problems arose that had catastrophic potential, I would see my dad fast and pray and put his confidence in God. I saw God bring him out of so many situations as a result of his faith that I find myself today reflecting back on what I've seen God do in his life. This gives me the assurance that by putting my confidence in Jesus Christ, He will not let me down. It is important that your children see you stand firmly in your faith. I did not realize that I was receiving a portion of my dad's faith just by being His son and observing his victories. I now live my life in a way that my four sons and daughter will use me one day as an example of someone who walks in complete confidence no matter what life's circumstances may bring.

So, if faith is transferable, that means fear is also transferable.

> *"For God hath not given us*
> *the spirit of fear, but of power,*
> *and of love, and of a sound mind."*
> *2 Timothy 1:7 (KJV)*

So take time to think about what you are transferring to your descendents—a spirit of fear or a spirit of faith.

Proactive Faith

Proactive: acting in anticipation of the future.
(Merriam-Webster Dictionary)

Another aspect of faith is *proactive faith*. This is the faith that begins to activate things in your life. It is the faith you need to really begin to move mountains in your life. It is what you are going to need to start having things work for your benefit. It is the kind of faith that will enable you to start reaching the unreachable and doing the impossible. It is the type of faith that charges and energizes you and will produce great things based on the word that you intake.

In order to put your faith in action you are going to need to experience solid preaching and teaching on a consistent basis. Therefore, it is important for you to have a good spiritual leader to pull you out of your past, push you out of your present, and cause you to live your future right now. Today, you can live your future because of proactive faith. Proactive faith works like this: whenever you hear the word of God, seeds are being sown into your heart, which is your spirit. This seed will encourage or influence you to start doing things that you thought you could never do. That is what a good preacher or teacher will do. He or she will put the word in you to cause you to expand your way of thinking. And once your mindset has expanded, the next step is to act on what you have heard.

Years ago, when I used to hang out in the club, I had a high top fade with a blond streak in the front. One day, I decided to use some "S curl." I was inexperienced with using it so I took the cream, put it in my hair, washed it out and it looked pretty decent, but not like the person on the box. I then saw a little bottle that said, "activator." It was not until I added the activator that I started getting the results that the product promised. That is why you must add works to your faith. When you put those two together, you cause the impossible to happen. What good is your faith until you start using it? What good is your faith until you put it in action? Faith is an action word that can only work when you apply it to every day life situations, especially when you do not have everything you need to get the job done. You may have only a little bit, but God knows what to do with a little. Just a little work, combined with your faith, makes the little much.

There are some things that you have been waiting on God to do, but God is waiting on you. It is not until you go out and act on it, that you will see results. There are people who wait for things to happen; people who watch things happen; and people who make things happen. In the book of John, chapter 5, there was a man who had an infirmity for thirty-eight years. He had an encounter with Jesus, who is the Word. When Jesus saw him, Jesus knew he had been with that condition for a long time. Jesus asked him a question, "Will you be made whole?" In response, the man said, "Every time I try to get in the pool, somebody steps in front of me, or there is no one to assist me." Jesus then tells the man to, "Rise, take up thy bed and walk." And immediately, that man was made whole because he took up his bed, and did what he thought he couldn't do. Wow! One word that he acted on made him accomplish what he thought he couldn't do in thirty-eight years.

So many times, we fail to activate our faith because we focus on thoughts such as: *I do not have any help; nobody cares about me or is looking out for me; I need assistance; everybody else has friends;* or *everybody else gets support.* Do not waste time waiting for people to help you when you can take your faith and put it into action. Instead of waiting around for help, follow the model in Romans, chapter 4, the word of God says that even God looked at the non-existing things and spoke to them as though they already existed. There is something very powerful in what you say. God looked upon the non-existent, spoke to it, and saw what He spoke. God said, "Let there be," and what He said became. You have to say it, and then see it. Every time I say something, I see something. You ought to speak better over yourself so that you can start seeing it.

In John 5:1-8, the man was so stuck in his tradition because it was customary for everyone to be healed one particular way. So he sat around thirty-eight years waiting for the same thing to happen for him the same way it did for everyone else. We cannot limit God based on the way He performs in other peoples' lives. Hebrews 12:1 (KJV) says, "… let us run with patience, the race that is set before us." Other translations use "course" that is set before us. I like to call it obstacle courses, because there are some obstacles that are designed for your life that may not be for someone else's life. Likewise, there are some obstacle courses that may be designed for someone else's life that may not be designed for your life. So run *your* course with patience. And by staying on your course, the glory of God can be achieved in your life. Remember, *your* course.

Do not wait in line for your change when you do not have to. Don't wait to be next. The moment you believe, you can be healed immediately. I do not want people to tell me that I am next in line for a miracle because that means I have to wait for someone else. When we hear the word, and understand that the word is seed, and that seed is no good unless it is planted, we must act. Our actions and response to the word determine how good our ground is, because our heart is our ground and the word is our seed. Therefore, the word, which falls on good ground, represents those who hear the word, keep it, and will bring forth much fruit with patience. I do not want to hear, "I am up next," because we are up the minute we believe and receive the word of God in our hearts. At that point, it is our time, and our moment to receive. I do not know when my moment is going to come, but I know that I am not going to get in line and wait behind someone else.

Have you ever been in a store and gotten into a slow line? Can you imagine if every blessing in your life was based on someone else getting theirs first? Someone may not be as progressive as you are. Thanks be unto God that He has given us the power to hear the word and then respond to what we hear. You do not have to wait in line for your breakthrough. It is instantaneous the moment you believe it in your heart and receive it! Because Jesus told the man at the pool of Bethesda to, "get up, take up thy bed and walk;" because he responded to Jesus' word *walk*, the power of faith, along with his actions, caused his healing.

When your season and day of appointment comes, nobody can get in your way or slow you down. You shall bring forth your fruit in your season. According to Psalm 1:3 (AMP), ". . . he shall be like a tree firmly planted [and tended] by the streams of water, ready to bring forth its fruit in its season; its leaf also shall not fade or wither; and everything he does shall prosper [and come to maturity]." And know this, nobody has to see your power, potential or recognize your anointing in order for it to be your time. When it is your time, you shall come forth.

Put your confidence in God. Everyone around you could be going through a drought, a depression, or even losing everything they have, and you can still blossom. God does not make your appointment based on the season or the economy. You are like a tree planted by the rivers of water. This tree that was planted, by the rivers of water, did not depend on the rainfall. Trees that are planted inland depend on the forecast, but trees planted by the river have a water supply all around them. So in case a drought comes, the tree that is planted by the river can still bloom while every other tree dries up. God has a way of getting blessings to you in spite of your surroundings. If God said it, He will perform it.

You have to know Him as the God of [*whatever your name is*]. Elijah needed people to know that God was the God of Elijah. I know Him as the God of Orrin.

Elijah wet the altar and prayed because he needed God to demonstrate His authority and power in his life in the presence of his enemies. Not only did God pour down fire from heaven to consume the altar, but He also consumed the false prophets of Baal. God is getting ready to show up in your life and demonstrate His power. Sometimes God will allow things to happen to you in public so that when He delivers, He turns your public shame into your public fame. God needs to use you to show the magnitude of His power. I know it is hard sometimes, when everybody is counting you out, but stop putting so much emphasis on your enemies that doubt your abilities.

A powerful man of God, who mentored me when I was eighteen years old, told me that the biggest payback to all my enemies was my success. So, he told me to just be successful. You hurt your enemies the most when you succeed in spite of what they say, in spite of the traps and snares they set, and in spite of their attempts to pull you down.

Make this confession now:

> "I CANNOT FAIL...
> I SHALL BE SUCCESSFUL."

Once you acknowledge your inherited faith and put it into action, there is another component you must have in your arsenal before you can reach unstoppable faith. That brings us to our next dimension of faith: Faith Knowing.

Faith Knowing

> *Knowing - to be aware of the truth or factuality of; be convinced or certain of.*
> (Merriam-Webster Dictionary)

The final aspect of faith is *faith knowing;* knowing who God is. To know means to perceive directly; to be acquainted or familiar with; to have experience of; to be aware of the truth or factuality of; to be convinced or certain of; to have a practical understanding of; or to have knowledge of.

In the past several sections, we have been talking about having a belief in and acting on that which is unseen. Now, however, we are shifting to the realm of knowing. Knowing is distinct from believing. The definition for believe is, "to put confidence in something or someone without actual proof." For example, if someone asked me, is Orrin Jr. my son, and I answered them, "I believe so," they would look at me and say, "What? You are not sure?" But because I know for sure that he is my son and I have evidence of my characteristics in him—and my gosh he looks just like me—to prove that he is my son, I do not have to operate in the belief realm. So, to believe is NOT to know. To believe is to put confidence in and not have concrete evidence. Since, however, you have seen God do many things in your life, have witnessed how He brought you in and out of life's circumstances and made ways for you, you ought to be fully persuaded and convinced of who God is and the power that He has in your life.

Shadrach, Meschach and Abed-Nego were so persuaded that God was able to deliver them from the fiery furnace that they would not bow down. They said, "Even if God does not deliver us, He is still able." You can only make statements like that when you have had some time and experience with God. I believe that you will reach the highest dimension of faith when you understand and know your God.

Another example of faith knowing can be seen in the life of David. David's greatest success was having a track record of the performance of God in his life. In I Samuel 17 (KJV), when David was preparing for one of the biggest battles in his life, the battle against the giant Philistine, Goliath, he was a young man who had not been militarily trained. His only reason for being at the battlefield at that time, when Goliath called the armies of Israel out to battle against him, was to bring his eldest brothers' food. David heard the cry of Goliath to choose a man to fight against him. All of Saul's specially trained military men were afraid of this giant. So David opened his mouth and said, "Who is this uncircumcised Philistine, that he should defy the armies of the living God?"

David is ready to jump in there and take Goliath out! Saul intervened, sent for David, and said, "He is a man of war from his youth. You are just a shepherd boy, David." And David said, "Saul, when I was in my father's field tending to his sheep, the lion came and the bear came and I destroyed the lion and the bear. This giant Philistine will not be any different." David was so convinced about the God that delivered him in the past that he did not even put on the armor that Saul offered him. David said to himself, "If God can deliver me from the lion and the bear, then He sure will deliver me from this Philistine." That is faith knowing. In order to obtain faith knowledge and walk in victory like David did and like Shadrach, Meschach, and Abednego did, you have to experience your share of suffering. Philippians 3:10 (KJV) says,

"...that I may know Him and the power of His resurrection and the fellowship of His sufferings, being made conformable unto His death."

The more suffering that we go through, the more we can identify with His suffering and His pains.

Romans 5:3-4 (KJV) says,

"And not only so, but we glory in tribulation also; knowing that tribulation worketh patience; and patience, experience; and experience, hope."

That experience, of which the writer speaks, is your experience with God. The more things you get into, and He pulls you out of, the more you know who God is and the more you experience His power.

Knowing God will help you with your daily walk and your confidence in Him. When you have experience with God, you will realize that,

"many are the afflictions of the righteous, but the Lord delivers him out of them all." Psalm 34:19 (NKJV)

When you know God, like Job knew Him, even the people you love will not be able to convince you to walk away from God because things are not going your way. Romans 8:35 (KJV) says,

"who shall separate us from the love of Christ? Shall tribulation, or

> *distress or persecution, or famine,*
> *or nakedness, or peril, or sword?"*

Verse 38-39 goes on to say,

> *"For I am persuaded that neither death,*
> *nor life, nor angels, nor principalities, nor powers,*
> *nor things present, nor things to come, nor height,*
> *nor depth, nor any other creature shall be*
> *able to separate us from the love of*
> *God, which is in Christ Jesus."*

The longer you walk with the Lord and suffer with the Lord, the more you will know Him.

The combination of a measure of faith, inherited faith, proactive faith, and faith knowing is critical to your being able to walk in unstoppable faith.

Perception

PERCEPTION

Your faith knowing, discussed in the last chapter, is enhanced by a quality called perception. Perception is your ability to comprehend or to discern. It means to detect, to recognize and to identify. Perception is how you view a thing.

A simple parable was once told to me, which you may have heard. If I have a glass of water, which is filled to the halfway mark, will I perceive that it is half full or half empty? Apply this principle to the way you look at your bank account(s). Are they half full or half empty? Your perception is important.

Some people are optimistic while others are pessimistic. Optimists say that it can be done, or it is possible. Pessimists have a negative outlook, insisting that it is impossible.

Perception is very important. When you can perceive properly, you can make the right decisions based on your level of discernment. Your perception gives you a visual of the outcome.

In Mark 5:39, Jesus needed the people in the house with Him to have the same perception that He had. This damsel, the ruler of the synagogue's daughter, was dead to everyone else. But Jesus' view was that she was only asleep. Some of the people in the house laughed at and mocked Jesus because their perception of His abilities was not where it should have been. As a result of the way they perceived the situation, in order for Jesus to perform this miracle, He had to eliminate everyone who did not have the same faith level that He had in order to get the job done. He put them out of the house and healed the damsel. Because Jesus knew the outcome, He was able to say, "She is not dead, just asleep." Perception empowers you to have a visual of the end in the beginning.

There have been many times in my life when I was connected to people that did not have the same faith level as I had. In order to keep them from laughing at me and discouraging me with their doubt, I would keep a lot of things that God would show me and instruct me to do to myself so that their negativity could not affect my progress. Could it be that some people that are around you are affecting your optimism, your zeal and your progress? Try to surround yourself with people that can see a better you, and want to see you succeed. Sometimes success comes when you are in a success-minded environment. The scripture says:

"For as he thinketh in his heart, so is he..."
Proverbs 23:7 (KJV)

Good perception will birth positive thinking, and positive thinking will protect your spirit and your emotions enabling you to handle hard times and bad circumstances. Good perception will also give you good conception. When I think of conception it always reminds me of the auto show. Every year auto makers will manufacture concept cars for the future. They are not ready to be sold but their concept of what cars would look like in the next 10-15 years offers a preview of what is to come. When you have good perception you will conceive ideas that will shape your life years ahead of time. It is what people refer to as, "living ahead of your time." I like to call it, "Living your future today," because good perception causes me to dress, conduct, and pattern my life based on what I see coming rather than what is here today. One thing that the enemy wants to do is cause you to live day by day. I know there are some songs that we sing such as, "One day at a time, sweet Jesus." But we as the body of Christ have to start planning to exist beyond our today. Every major Fortune 500 company has already planned today how they are going to make their next billion dollars years from now. So, good perception causes you to plan for your future. You must plan today to exist tomorrow. You will not be here tomorrow by accident, but by destiny. So start preparing now for your future success.

The woman in 2 Kings 4:8-10 had some kind of perception from the beginning, before she expressed it to her husband. She said every time the prophet passed through she would make accommodations for him. She knew there was something different about Elisha. Her perception caused her to respond to him in ways that she would not respond to any other man. She pointed out that he was holy. Because she had good perception, she invested in what she perceived. She asked her husband to make provision for the man of God because she perceived that he was holy. When you have good perception, you are willing to take the risk and invest. Think about this: A married woman convinced her husband to let another man stay in their house just because she had insight about who he was.

> *"And she said unto her husband, Behold now, I perceive this is a holy man of God, which passeth by us continually."*

Then, she made provisions for her perception.

> *"Let us make a little chamber, I pray thee, on the wall; and let us set for him there a bed, and a table, and a stool, and a candlestick: and it shall be, when he cometh to us, that he shall turn in thither."*
> 2 Kings 4:9-10 (KJV)

When you are set apart and chosen there is something about you that causes people to be drawn to that side of you. It is not about how well you dress, or the amount of money you have, because none of that is important. What is important is for people to see the God in you. When people perceive God in your life they will bend over backwards to help you. Elisha wasn't hiding his relationship with his God. Elisha wasn't keeping his relationship with God private. Something about his attitude and lifestyle commanded this level of attention. This woman had not known Elisha for a long period, however, her perception caused her to respond positively. The Bible says to, "try the spirit by the spirit."

"Beloved, believe not every spirit, but try the spirits whether they are of God: because many false prophets are gone out into the world. "
1 John 4:1 (KJV)

If you start testing spirits from the beginning, there are certain relationships that you will avoid.

In 2 Kings 4:10, we know that the Shunamite woman is doing all of this for the man of God based on perception, because the scripture does not mention any prior relationship or fellowship, just PERCEPTION. She obviously got her husband's consent. Her husband either trusted his wife's relationship with God or he himself perceived Elisha to be a man of God.

Jesus said, "… flesh and blood hath not revealed this to you." (Matthew 16:17) You cannot always go by flesh and blood to get a correct diagnostic of a person or personality. You have to rely on the spirit of God that is within you to connect with the spirit of God in another person in order to bring about full perception. In other words, do not get married until you perceive correctly. Do not link up with your next friend, associate or business partner until you perceive correctly.

Good Perception Yields Positive Manifestations

The woman received favor for taking good care of Elisha by feeding him whenever he passed through. Finally, in 2 Kings 4:12, he asked her what he could do for her because she had been a blessing to him.

> *"And he said to Gehazi his servant,*
> *Call this Shunamite. And when he had called her,*
> *she stood before him. And he said unto him,*
> *Say now unto her, Behold, thou hast been careful*
> *for us with all this care; what is to be done for thee?*
> *Wouldest thou be spoken for to the king, or to*
> *the captain of the host? And she answered,*
> *I dwell among mine own people. And he said,*
> *What then is to be done for her? And Gehazi*
> *answered, Verily she hath no child,*
> *and her husband is old."*
> *2 Kings 4:12-14 (KJV)*

Because the Shunamite woman's perception of Elisha was accurate, she was granted the favor of the Lord. Her husband was old and she was unable to have children. But because she allowed her good perception to cause her to invest in what she perceived to be true about Elisha, blessings were released in her life because she made an investment in her perception. When you really have the power to perceive, it will cause you to believe in your own spiritual insight to discern, judge and make good choices in your life.

Overcoming Negative Perception

Often times, Christians have trouble maintaining a positive outlook concerning their lives and God's promises to them. This is primarily due to the negative seeds which were planted in them at some point in their lives. Those who were raised in unsaved homes where abuse and neglect were present, those who were in bad relationships or those who have experienced great tragedies and failures have often struggled with their faith and the hope that God's glory can, in spite of everything, manifest in their lives. You can overcome the negative perceptions that have been buried deep within you.

When you consistently pray and meditate on God's word and His promises concerning you, you can begin to uproot the negative lies and replace them with the positive and true word of God. As you change the way you think, you will change the words you speak and thus change your outlook on life. Your faith will increase and you will experience positive results in every area of your life.

Remembering Luke's gospel, chapter 5, there were some fishermen who had been fishing all night and caught absolutely nothing. When Jesus saw them they were washing out their nets and packing up. Jesus used their boat and taught for a short time and when He finished teaching, He told them to launch out into the deep for a haul. Simon Peter said to Jesus,

"...Master, we have toiled all the night, and have taken nothing: nevertheless at thy word I will let down the net."
Luke 5:5 (KJV)

Simon made this statement based on his past negative experience but he was able to overcome because he put it in the hands of Jesus. He uses the word, "nevertheless" because now it was based on Jesus' word and not Simon's past experience.

How many times have we allowed our past experiences to cause us not to try again or to go back again? But when you have unstoppable faith, you won't let past failures hinder you from trying again. Tell me, "No," but that won't stop me. Tell me, "I can't," but that won't stop me. Tell me it's beyond my abilities, that won't stop me because there is a God who is able to do exceeding abundantly above all that I could ask or think according to the power that worketh in me. The power that should be working in us is the power of faith and when you've really got it, nothing will stop you. Now let's look at the results of God's word being greater than Simon Peter's past experience:

> *"And when they had this done, they inclosed a great multitude of fishes: and their net brake."*
> *Luke 5:6 (KJV)*

God's word is greater than your past failures. Simon Peter received above and beyond his expectations. Because he trusted in Jesus, his net broke as a result of the abundance he received.

That is what we are looking for in our various situations—results, the favor of God, answers to our prayers, and the manifestation of the promises God has made to us. Replacing negative perception with right perception can help us achieve all of that. Right perception can help move us from promise to possession.

From Promise to Possession
How do we get there?

FROM PROMISE TO POSSESSION:
How do we get there?

There are some God given principles that take you from promise to possession. Enough of dreaming or envisioning it, now it is time to grasp and take hold of what God has spoken over your life. As you continue going through the process of unstoppable faith, there is something that will shift for you and increase your faith level to move you from promise to possession. You are going to start obtaining the things that you believe God for and the things that God has spoken over your life. God has some laws that govern possession and manifestation. In order to possess the promises of God, there are a number of principles you must follow and attitudes you must have. Those will be discussed in this chapter.

<u>Receive and Accept It</u>

One of the keys to obtaining the manifestation of what God has promised is receiving and accepting the promise. In John 17:8 (AMP) Jesus is talking to the Father and saying:

"For the [uttered] words that You gave Me I have given them; and they have received and accepted [them] and have come to know positively and in reality [to believe with absolute assurance] that I came forth from Your presence, and they have believed and are convinced that You did send Me."

You have to receive and accept God's word and plan for your life.

Many times, we receive something but then we do not accept it. Some of us say to ourselves, "I heard what was said, I understand it, but I do not know how that is going to happen in my life." We do not accept that it is going to happen. We have to, as the disciples did in John 17:8 (AMP), "come to know positively and in reality [to believe with absolute assurance]."

One way that you can help this process is by reading, studying, and listening to the Word of God. Romans 10:17 (KJV) says,

"...faith cometh by hearing and hearing by the word of God."

It is important for you to hear the word in order to believe, to receive and to accept. I get greater power and ability in God whenever I start reading and studying His word. Do not allow anything else to move you, except the Word. The Word is that which will bring you to a place of completion and fulfillment!

Obedience

In addition to receiving and accepting the promise, one must also learn how to be obedient to God and to His voice. God gives us orders and a plan. Then we have to be faithful to obey the orders and plans whether we feel God or not. For example, at one time in my life, God spoke to me and told me to pray every morning at 6:00 a.m. As such, I must pray at 6:00 a.m. until God changes the plan. Even though right now God may speak to you all of the time, there will come a time when you may not feel or hear Him. This is when you have to understand that God has given you a promise and a plan. You must be obedient to the voice of God no matter what you are facing.

In Genesis 22:16-17, Abraham goes from a promise to possession as he obeys the voice of God. First, he has to have enough faith to get a son and then he has to obey God when He says to offer his son, Isaac, up as a burnt sacrifice. Abraham remains obedient.

You have to realize sometimes that some promises are seeds to other promises. Once we are able to obtain one promise, sometimes He will challenge us to take the promise and use it for His glory. Sometimes we are tempted to say, "Well God, You gave me this. You promised this to me and it took me all this time to get it so I am going to hold onto the promise that You gave." Okay, but what about your next level?

There is nothing that my wife and I did out of abundance. We always gave out of a sacrifice on our current level, putting ourselves under the care of God for the next level. In everything we do, we trust God for it. It is not as if money is flowing over and busting out of the seams. When we get to one level God always challenges us and says, "Now that you have reached this level, take what you received from this level and push to your next level." That is the problem with a lot of us. We get blessed and then we get stuck. Just like past failures can hinder future successes, so can small successes hinder greater successes. We get so blessed and then satisfied but maybe the level of blessings that we're on today is not the greatest level that God has designed for our lives. I have seen so many people succeed in something and get so overwhelmed with that one success that they are not willing to go any further. Abraham's son, Isaac, was a promised seed-singular, but when God saw Abraham's obedience to sacrifice his seed, He promised Abraham that he would be the recipient of seeds-plural that number the sands of the sea and the stars in the sky.

> *"Then the Angel of the LORD called unto Abraham out of heaven the second time, And said, By myself have I sworn, saith the LORD, for because thou hast done this thing, and hast not withheld thy son, thine only son:*

*That in blessing I will bless thee,
and in multiplying I will multiply thy
seed as the stars of the heaven, and as the
sand which is upon the sea shore; and thy
seed shall possess the gate of his enemies;*

*And in thy seed shall all the nations of the earth
be blessed; because thou hast obeyed my voice."
Genesis 22:15-18 (KJV)*

I call this sowing the promise-singular for the promises-plural. Abraham and Sarah waited all those years for their promised seed, Isaac. He finally receives Isaac and God challenges him to sacrifice him as a burnt offering. Abraham obeys and the Lord sees his obedience and moves him from the promise to promises.

Some people do not like the pressure of possession because sometimes you have to sacrifice this level for the next. Once some people get financially stable, they stop right there and say "I am doing well now," in fear that they will return to their place of lack. I am here to encourage you, however, not to let fear stop you from going to your next level. Abraham took the promise of this level, his son Isaac, and sowed to his next level. Because he was willing to sow Isaac, not only would he be the father of Isaac, but the father of all of them that would believe. That one seed caused God to multiply his descendants. Your next level is based on the seed you sow. If you want unlimited seed and harvest, sow what you received on this level so that you can reach the next level of promise that God has for you.

It takes major faith in God to get to a place where you are able to hear and obey God even when it does not make sense. Sometimes that which God says does not make sense to your human reason and understanding and He does not have to. His thoughts are far beyond your thoughts. His ways are far above your ways.

"For my thoughts are not your thoughts, neither are your ways my ways, saith the LORD."

"For as the heavens are higher than the earth, so are my ways higher than your ways,

> *and my thoughts than your thoughts."*
> *Isaiah 55:8-9 (KJV)*

It is good when God tells you something that does not make sense because that lets you know that He is God. If He is thinking on your level, then He cannot be God. If God thought on your level then it would keep you stuck where you are, but God is thinking about you in a greater way than what you are thinking about yourself. If you are worshipping the true and living God, He wants to thrust you to another level. In order for Him to do this, you have to obey God and invest your today into your tomorrow.

Holiness

In addition to obedience, we must walk in holiness if we want to obtain the promises of God. God must possess us before we can possess His promises. Are you the Lord's possession? Does He have reign and rule over you? Does He have the rights to you? Some of us God has the rights to as long as we are going through and broke, but the minute we come out and become successful, we get independent of God, His church and everything about Him. I admonish you to continue to keep and understand the strategies that brought us out before. It is going to be that same strategy that allows us to maintain. I will say it again: God must possess us before we can possess His promises.

> *"Ye shall therefore keep all my statutes, and all my judgments, and do them: that the land, whither I bring you to dwell therein, spue you not out. And ye shall not walk in the manners of the nation, which I cast out before you: for they committed all these things, and therefore I abhorred them.*
>
> *But I have said unto you, Ye shall inherit their land, and I will give it unto you to possess it, a land that floweth with milk and honey: I am the LORD your God, which have separated you from other people.*
>
> *Ye shall therefore put difference between clean beasts and unclean, and between unclean fowls and clean: and ye shall not make your souls abominable by beast, or by fowl, or by any manner of living thing*

> *that creepeth on the ground, which*
> *I have separated from you as unclean.*
>
> *And ye shall be holy unto me:*
> *for I the LORD am holy, and have*
> *severed you from other people."*
> *Leviticus 20:22-26 (KJV)*

Verse 24 is about sanctification. God has set you apart from other people. The next verse talks about being different, meaning there should be a distinction between the world and us. There should be a distinction between being rich and prosperous. You see, the world can only depend on riches, but we depend on prosperity because prosperity is good health, wealth, peace and rejoicing in each of them.

God is looking to bless distinction. He is not looking to bless someone who is common and following this world's system and guidelines for success. You do not have to gain success the way everyone else does because God wants you to be distinct and unique. He wants to show you off by bringing you out of poverty into a wealthy place. The distinction between the rich person who walked into an inheritance and you is that God alone can get the glory out of your success.

Some people look at their achievements and become conceited. This is easy to see in corporate America. Too many people begin to view themselves more importantly than they should. Instead of glorifying God, they brag on their credentials. If you ask them how they made it, they will credit their Ivy-league degrees for their success. When you get the car that you desire, make sure that the world knows that Jesus is your source. A degree does not mean automatic success. I know this, because I have seen many people working jobs for which they are overqualified. There are many people with Master's degrees working at Rite Aid, Walgreen's, K-Mart, etc.

We have to understand that God wants to bless us, but He has to put distinction between the world and us. Do not criticize me because I put *Tither* or *Blessed of God* on my license plate. I need the world to know to whom I am connected. It is not by my own power or abilities that I got this wealth, but it is the Lord's doing. Do not be ashamed of your identity in God or change when God blesses you. Let the world know that it was Jesus.

Continually giving God the glory for the success in your life goes along with what I said earlier, that we must be God's possessions before He can give us His promises. When we belong to Him, then we are ready to receive His blessings.

There were people that entered into places illegally, but as soon as they hit the digestive system of the land they entered, it vomited them out (Leviticus 20:22). If you are corrupt and try to be successful in God, then your prosperity will last only for a moment. Your car will vomit you out, your new house will vomit you out, your marriage will vomit you out. Eventually, God is going to spit you out. This is why you often see people rise up quickly and then fall, because the land was one of purity and promise and could no longer keep them in the system. It had to spit them back out. You do not want to be up today and down tomorrow.

Unfortunately, many people are living this type of lifestyle. Everything seems to be going well for them, but then all of a sudden things begin to go haywire. This is because something is vomiting them up. It is just like someone being promoted illegally and it lasts for only six months or so. Sometimes you see God bless and perform a miracle for someone and think you can copy him or her and get into something that you cannot afford. Whether it is a car, house, club membership or any other great expenditure, expect it to not to work.

Also know that when your character or attitudes are displeasing to God, you can expect to part with your success quickly. There are some people that will start mistreating others once they achieve success.

By the time you get to where God wants to take you, you will know how to handle the blessing and how to treat others. If you think things are out of place in my life, then either you should help me or keep quiet, because God is not through with me yet. Some people are not ready for God to bless them. God knows that if He blesses some people where they are, they would start to look down on others. I cannot understand people that are uppity and yet have nothing. Could you imagine what they would do if God gave them a little wealth?

The Lord is looking to bless those who will represent His kingdom. He is looking for someone to be distinguished and to represent the difference between right and wrong. This is our time as the body of Christ. God is restoring order and favor in His body. All of the overnight wonders that popped up proclaiming to be leaders, and who degraded the office, will be replaced by ordained and consecrated vessels. How can you be a leader and not be an example of one? You cannot even keep your marriage together. True leaders will walk in line with the qualifications of the office. Many leaders are throwing their spouses away and getting new ones. All I can say is you are illegal and your empire is coming to an end. Do not be deceived because some leaders are sitting in a chair, because it is just a chair. They still do not have any power or authority. It is just like Saul. While he was yet sitting on his throne, God was raising up David in the land. In this hour,

God is dethroning the spirit of Saul. Saul represents leaders that are selected by people and David was a leader selected by God.

Now, God is drawing up a leader from the House of Israel, one that He selects. God is bringing value back to the offices of Bishop, Pastor and Prophet. When you walk in your office as a leader, do not prostitute it for money. If God spoke a word to someone, give it to them regardless of the amount of money they have, if any at all. Give them the word.

Where are the prophets like Jeremiah that did not preach for money or Elijah that did not care whether money was involved? God is raising up men and women who will love their spouses, not those who are living riotously and claiming to be leaders. God is restoring value back to the body of Christ and we are not going to be ashamed to tell people that we belong to Him. Know that you are valuable!

"And ye shall be holy unto me: for I the LORD am holy, and have severed you from other people, that ye should be mine."
Leviticus 20:26 (KJV)

God warns us of a people that currently possess the land. There are people currently in possession of your land, anointing, office, ministry and property, but God is getting ready to cross His hands. He is getting ready to shift the body of Christ in such a way that it is going to shake the very foundations of all the charlatans and imposters. He is going to cause a generation of people to rise up who will love Him, worship Him, and be true to His word. God has let some people walk in offices and places, but that place is getting ready to eject them. Galatians 6:9 says not to be weary in well doing for in due season you shall reap if you faint not. Do not fret because of evildoers, for in due season they shall be cut off. (Psalm 37:1-2) If you are not in right standing with God, now is the time to get right, and quickly. God is cutting people off and moving others into position.

"If you live in me [abide vitally united to Me] and My words remain in you and continue to live in your hearts,

*ask whatever you will,
and it shall be done for you."*
John 15:7 (AMP)

You are His possession and because He is in you, now He can trust you to walk into your promise.

I want to tell you that after reading this book, when you lay the old life down this time you will never ever take it back up again! When Jesus said, "No man will take my life, but I lay it down," He is not talking about this life here on earth. The life that I am going to lay down here in the natural, I will never pick up again. But the life outside this flesh, my life seated in heavenly places at the right hand of God Almighty, that is the life Jesus was going to take back—the real life. If you keep having the problem of falling down, getting back up and falling down again, I want to tell you that when you make a conscious decision to die to your flesh, you will be changed forever. And my friend, holiness is the beginning of your prosperity. It is the beginning of your manifested life in Jesus Christ. The lifestyle that you are getting ready to pick up now is a brand new life in

Jesus Christ. It is the real life—the good life. It is beneficial to you because now you have a Heavenly lineage. I let go of the lineage of my mom and dad in the natural world and took on the lineage of Jesus Christ, Abraham, Isaac and Jacob. Now I will receive the blessings and inheritance of my spiritual lineage through Jesus Christ. This is the Zoe or God kind of life.

In order for the fullness of God's glory to be revealed in your life, you have to start hating the world. The Bible says that you cannot be Christ's disciples and still love the world and worldly things, but you have to give your life and lay it down completely. Laying down your life requires an inner self-breaking. You break your own spirit; lose your opinion and emotions and say, "Lord I give you everything." I do not lay down my life to somebody who will do me in." When you first were saved, you did not stop partying at the club because somebody made you. You chose to lay down your life of club hopping and decided to live your life in the house of God. It was a choice that you made.

Has anyone told you that you are wasting your time living for God? Nobody made you start tithing. Nobody made you start sowing seed. It was a choice you made because you realized that you wasted a lot of money in the world on alcohol, dancing and ungodly relationships. But you decided to lay your life down. Nobody made you do it.

When Jesus talked about laying His life down, He was talking about this natural life right here on earth and this lifestyle in this human body. Jesus said in verse 18 of John 10 that "no man has taken it away, I have the power to lay it down." It seems that He is saying, "I am going to lay it down and then take it back," because that is sometimes what we do. We give up our old ways for a moment, but the minute we want to get it back we take it back again.

I remember when I was sixteen and had just given my heart to Jesus. I was at a family dinner and my brothers aggravated me so badly that I said, "Let us step outside." My sister said, "You are saved, right?" I said, "Yes, but these fists do not change." You see, I conveniently laid down my life saying, "Oh Lord, I love you, I praise You," but as soon as somebody provoked me, I picked my old life back up. That is not holiness and that is not the path to access the promises of God. Being set apart, distinctive, unique, and forsaking that which is displeasing to God—being holy—puts us on the path toward possessing the promises of God.

Confidence

The third thing we must have in order to possess is confidence. We must be assured of the promises of God. (Numbers 13:27-30) When Moses sent out spies to survey the land, some came back saying, "Oh Moses, we cannot do it. The people are big over there, and they are giants." They said, "We are grasshoppers in their sight and even in our own sight." Then here comes Caleb who is of another mind. He quiets the people by telling them that they were well able to possess and conquer the land. There are many days of the week that I have to tell myself that I am well able and that I will not fall apart or break under pressure. The promises are not just going to be handed to you. Now is the time for you to go up and start possessing some things. Say to yourself, "I am well able and must go at once to possess what God promised."

Your confidence must be built upon Jesus Christ.

> *"Let us hold fast the profession of our faith without wavering; (for he is faithful that promised)"*
> *Hebrews 10:23 (KJV)*

We have to do this without fluctuating. Our confession cannot be wishy-washy. *"He can. No, He cannot. He can. No, He cannot."* Understand that profession is openly declaring or publicly claiming. The problem now is that many of us do not have a profession anymore.

Profession means to openly make a statement by faith concerning something that is to come. Are you willing to be embarrassed if it does not happen? You have to get so bold that you do not care who knows about it because the promise belongs to you. Many times we have quiet confessions, but God is looking for some men and women who are not afraid to decree and declare what our God is able to do. Look at Elijah and the prophets of Baal. The prophet Elijah declared what God would do. He declared Heaven's fire to come down and consume the altar. Are you confident enough about your God? Your victory? Your promise? That vision you are holding onto, are you certain that it came from God and not some random dream? If God spoke a thing in your life, you should not be afraid to profess it! Your profession will bring about possession. That is one of our God qualities: to say a thing and receive a thing. In Genesis, chapter 1, God said, "Let there be," and there was.

> *"Therefore I say unto you, What things soever ye desire, when ye pray, believe that ye receive them, and ye shall have them."*
> *Mark 11:24 (KJV)*

Profess your way into your promise. I am speaking my victory and my breakthrough. I am professing that I will not be broke another day because God promises in His word that He shall supply all my need. You need to be making some professions:

I AM A WEALTHY CHILD OF GOD;
MY CHILDREN ARE WEALTHY;
MY HOUSE IS WEALTHY;
EVERYTHING AROUND ME IS WEALTHY.

Even though you may be going through a little dilemma, you do not have to waver. If God says He is going to increase your business, then your business is increased and everything is well. Do not despise small beginnings because if you keep professing that, "this shall grow and it shall be large and it shall be great," then greatness has to come because you are willing to profess. When you profess, you put your God on the spot. God is well able.

From obedience to holiness, from holiness to confidence, from confidence to self-control, He is faithful.

Self-Control

Self-control is one of the things that we lack sometimes. You should have enough self-control to wait on God and put your confidence in Him and not accept anything less than what God promised you. Do not lose it when things go wrong. Have self-control. That means you are going to keep your *self* on course until God turns it around. You have to practice self-control. Control your emotions and stop letting your feelings take over your choices and decisions. Sometimes in order to control yourself, you have to talk to yourself. There were many days when just talking to myself kept me under control. Sometimes I would say, "Orrin, just shut up because if you say something it is going to go to the next level." Self-control comes by way of the Holy Spirit. Some people say things like, "If they mess with me, I am going to give them a piece of my mind." You should not wait until people upset you to tell them the truth. Self-control from the Holy Spirit will tell you to keep quiet and hold your peace. God wants to make you stable in personality, emotions and faith.

Patience

Luke 8:15 (KJV) says,

"But that on the good ground are they, which in an honest and good heart, having heard the word, keep it, and bring forth fruit with patience."

Patience is perfecting something in you. Let delays and extended long periods develop you, because sometimes God does not come right away. You may have called on God, begging Him to deliver you from your circumstance, and it seemed that He failed to respond. It may even seem to you that things are getting worse. You have to know that God is stretching you and increasing your capacity. Besides, as 2 Corinthians 4:17 (KJV) says,

"For our light affliction, which is but for a moment, worketh for us a far more exceeding and eternal weight of glory."

The reason He has to stretch you is because when the blessings come to hit your life you have to have enough capacity for the weight of the promise.

Your promises are coming heavy. God is not doing a light thing in this hour, but He is doing something heavy.

> *"For ye have need of patience, that, after ye have done the will of God, ye might receive the promise."*
> *Hebrews 10:36 (KJV)*

Patience is directly connected to obtaining the promises of God. God may be trying to teach you patience because your temper is too short. Do not get angry when things do not happen right away. When patience is complete then will patience have her perfect work and you will be whole (James 1:4). God wants to do a thorough job with you. Do not settle for a rush job. You may want things to happen for you instantly, but God says, "I have to do a thorough job." He wants to make sure that you know how to handle the blessings.

Patience means to wait on God for the results or return. Results do not always come instantly. Sometimes it takes time and patience.

You cannot bring forth fruit without patience. You cannot plant a seed and expect it tomorrow. It takes patience to water, fertilize and nurture your seed. John 12:24 (KJV) says, "Verily, verily I say unto you, except a corn of wheat fall into the ground and die, it abideth alone; but if it die, it bringeth forth much fruit." Do not rush what God is doing. There are some things in your life that must die. Some ways about you must die before you can receive your harvest. You will bring forth a hundred fold if you practice patience. Give yourself time for God to develop a strong foundation in you.

Sometimes in your haste, you can rush that seed right out of the ground. You can plant seed one day and then go dig it up the next. You must let it go through its course. When you trust God, you will not operate out of desperation. Doubt will cause you to make some desperate moves and choices and put you into some compromising relationships and situations. There were some things, for example, that I wanted God to do in my first two years of pastoring. I wanted the church to be overflowing and I wanted a great budget to do the work of the Lord. However, that early in ministry, I was not ready. If God had given it to me when I wanted it, I know I would have made a mess of it. I had to be processed first. Then after a level of maturity came into my life, I experienced one open door after the next. So, embrace the delay because in God's timing He will do everything He has promised.

When you wait on God, you do not have to be desperate. The Holy Spirit will give you enough confidence to endure the delays. Wait on your harvest and do not give up. God is going to do everything that He told you. Not just some of it is coming to pass, but all of it. Every promise, every prophetic word, every dream, every vision shall come to pass in due season.

> *Due: having reached the date at which payment is required; expected to give birth.*
> (Merriam-Webster Dictionary)

The Bible says in Habakkuk that the vision is yet for an appointed time. When your due season comes, there is nothing the enemy or anyone else can do to stop you from receiving payment. You've got to know that you have a due date--a date of expectation. It is like being pregnant with child. After nine months has passed, that baby has to come out no matter what. After your season of development you have to bring forth everything that has been seeded inside of you. Get excited! Keep your head up. Your due season is ahead of you.

Being Content in Lack

In addition to needing holiness, obedience, confidence, self-control, and patience in order to possess the promises of God, there are certain attitudes and mindsets that you must develop before you possess the promise.

One attitude that must come before receipt of the promise is being content in lack.

> *"Not that I speak in respect of want:*
> *for I have learned, in whatsoever state*
> *I am, therewith to be content."*
> *Philippians 4:11 (KJV)*

God used lack to stretch me so far that when blessings came my way, I did not become conceited. I was able to receive the blessings with a clear head. You will not understand or appreciate blessings until you can appreciate lack. God teaches you how to appreciate the little things. Fifty dollars means something to me, because I know how hard it was to obtain it at one point in my life. There are times when God has to teach you lack. He allows you to suffer for a long time so that when your change comes, you will know how to handle the blessings of God.

The reason I can be content in lack is because my faith gives me the power to not focus on my current status, but rather to focus on my future expectation date. In doing so, I continue to stay constant with God. I remain what I have been—steadfast and immovable—knowing that God is going to change my circumstances.

Do you know how to walk in lack and still keep a prayer life? Can you suffer lack and still love your enemies? Do you know how to walk in lack and still appreciate people that are doing well and not get jealous of their blessings? You may have been down as far as you can go, but when your day of deliverance arrives, you need to know how to rejoice and give God the praise. Can you see your future; your breakthrough; the dawning of a new day? When you come out of this, you are going to know that God is well able to do the impossible, to do exceeding abundantly above all that you could ever think or imagine!

Be Flexible

Finally, if we are going to possess the promises of God, we have to be flexible. When God gave me my wife, He customized her for me. I have to celebrate my wife and encourage other brothers to celebrate their wives. I did not deserve this kind of woman, but His grace and mercy brought me places I did not deserve to be and possessions I did not deserve to have. I want to make sure that you are walking in divine destiny and not just putting something that God gave you to the side. You have to take care of and protect your investment.

You must be flexible when it comes to the things of God. Things do not always have to go your way as long as God is going to give you the victory at the end. Gideon started out with 32,000 men and ended up with 300. He was already short with 32,000, yet God caused him to defeat his enemy with only 300. You must be flexible to change. Sometimes less is more. I tell my congregation all of the time, "You may not know the income but you must know the outcome is what God desires." Whenever God told me to do something, I did not know everything I was going to have to go through at the start. But if it is from God, I know that at the end He will make a way. If it is God's will it is God's bill. You must be flexible and yielded to whomever God wants to use, and whatever way God wants to take you, even when you do not understand.

Sometimes my wife and I have conversations about what we need from each other. Often times, we have to sit down, talk and go over some things in order to stay in tune with each other. I have to be flexible and understand that what worked for me years ago may not work for me today. The woman I married when I was in my twenties is not the same woman that I am married to now at 34. She was a different woman and I was a different man. Jesus is the only one who remains the same yesterday, today and forever. When I first married my wife, I could have promised her a house on the moon and she would have been so happy. But now, eleven years later, she will say to me, "Forget the moon. I'll take a house right here on this block." We do change, and because of this, we have to know how to go back to the floor of negotiations and renew the contract.

The problem with many couples is that they are trying to operate in the old system, not realizing that their spouse has changed. I have to deal with my wife differently as a successful woman versus the little girl I married because needs and desires change. This is why it is important to keep your marriage synchronized and to stay in the timing of your marriage. The more you grow and develop in your marriage, the more you will appreciate the smaller things. It may not have mattered years ago, but the smaller things are what matter nowadays. Taking time and making an impartation into what God has given you is important. Get your pride out of the way and say, "Honey, I want to be a good husband to you." "Baby I want to be a good wife to you." I think it is a foolish man who cannot [refuses to] be flexible.

If we are going to possess the promises of God, there are certain principles that we must follow and certain attitudes that we must develop. Our unstoppable faith works for us when we combine flexibility with our holiness, obedience, confidence, self-control, patience, and contentment, in whatsoever state we find ourselves.

The Predestined You

THE PREDESTINED YOU

Predestined: to destine, decree, determine, appoint, or settle beforehand.
(Merriam-Webster Dictionary)

As a believer, every promise is already sown into your spirit. It is sown into your predestination. Every ingredient about you is already foreordained. In the book of Genesis, when God created the Earth, the Earth existed. God then separated the dry ground from the waters and when it came time for all of the trees, grass, flowers and other plants to manifest, the Lord said, "Let the Earth bring forth grass yielding seed and fruit after its kind." When God made the Earth, He made the Earth complete and whole. Everything that the Earth needed to be Earth, was already in it. You have a head and you do not have to pray for hair because hair just comes. When God made your head, He put capabilities in your head to possess hair. The Earth was responsible for its part. There are things that you are responsible for that God has already put in you–abilities and capabilities. Within you is everything you need to begin. To be the predestined you, the manifested you, everything is already there. There is some stuff you are waiting on and being impatient with God about and God is saying, "I have given it to you already; bring forth. Now bring all the good out of you that I have placed and predestined in you."

The Earth has to bring forth everything that is already seeded inside of it. Every time the word is spoken, there is seed that is already inside of you that must come forth. There will come a time when you have to start bringing forth the seed or you will just be full of dreams, full of desires and full of visions, but no manifestation. Seed is meant to be planted and to produce. When it takes root in your ground, it cannot do anything but spring up. Some of you may be waiting for possession and waiting on God to do something and He is saying, "No, I need you to take action," because He has already given you the capabilities to do it.

Some of you just have to try. You will never possess it until you make an aggressive attempt. God will allow people to turn you down and refuse to give you help. If everybody helps you with everything you do then you will not know your own capabilities. There were times when I called to get help from others and could not reach them. That is when I began to depend less on people. I realized then that I would have to rely on myself and God to do what I needed to get done. I began to work the creative abilities that God placed inside of me. It was a blessing because I began to discover my own gifts, capabilities, talents and skills.

Sometimes you may want a handout so much that you do not really know what you have, especially when people, like your parents, always baby you. It is a terrible thing to be a grown man, forty years old, saying things like, "I am going back home." My Mom put me out when I was in my early teens because I was laying in the bed until 2:00 in the afternoon. She would storm into the room and say, "It is time to wake up! You cannot sleep all day!" I would say, "I am not going to school and I am not going to work." I would hang out at night and sleep all day. My

Mom used to say, "You got to get up out of here with your lazy self!" I thought she was joking around until I went out one night, came back and the locks were changed. Some parents need to change the locks and teach their children how to be adults. It helped me to be responsible because I no longer had the support of Mom and Dad. I had to be big enough to stand on my own. It used to be that if I did not work, I could ask my dad for money. I had a roof over my head, however, when I was out on my own, I had to learn to respect authority. When my boss was a little mean with me, I had to listen so that I would not be fired. I knew that not having a job meant not being able to eat and pay my rent. But when I was living at home, I would go from one job to the next because I knew my mom and dad had my back. That is a good thing, but not all of the time, because now, without the support of people, I can't give up. I have to remain determined in my efforts.

The Unstoppable You

THE UNSTOPPABLE YOU

<u>Unstoppable</u>: incapable of being stopped.
(Merriam-Webster Dictionary)

My friends, you must know what God has for you; what He has shown you and told you. You must have a strong determination to be everything that God has purposed for you to be. To be determined means to decide, to resolve, to take a position. You must make a decision that you cannot fail, but you will be successful.

In the book of Genesis, Isaac had a word of promise that was spoken to his father, Abraham, that he would be blessed. He fell upon major resistance in Genesis 26, because the Philistines stopped up and filled with dirt all the wells that his father had dug. And because Isaac was so blessed, resistance came automatically. When you are blessed, you automatically attract problems. I like to call it, "destiny attractions." There are certain spirits that often attract themselves to you when you have been purposed from God — the spirits of jealously, envy, strife and hatred.

"But he shall receive an hundredfold now in this time, houses, and brethren, and sisters, and mothers, and children, and lands, with persecutions; and in the world to come eternal life."
Mark 10:30 (KJV)

Jesus promised His disciples all of these blessings but He also included persecutions because with blessings comes problems. So your blessings attract enemies.

Abimelech spoke to Isaac in verse 16 and said, "Move away from us. You have become too powerful for us." Isaac understood and received the promise of his inheritance. As believers, we must first *receive* the promise of our spiritual inheritance. We must receive the promise of our natural inheritance right here on Earth now. Resistance must come once you understand and have a determination about where you are going. Isaac reopened the wells that had been dug in the time of his father and the Philistines stopped them up. Isaac had a word from God concerning location; that God would lead him to a place where he would be blessed. Yes, where you live and where you are located is very important. If you are going to grow oranges and have an orange farm, upstate New York is not a good location for that type of vision. Georgia and Florida, that is another story, because the climate is conducive for that kind of harvest. Therefore, you want to be sure that you are in a place that will bring forth the harvest that God wants you to produce. And God will give you direction. Psalms 23:2 (KJV) said: "He maketh me to lie down in green pastures. He leadeth me beside the still waters." So He leads us in the natural. Verse 3 says, "He leadeth me in the paths of righteousness," and in the spiritual. God will lead if we will submit and follow. Isaac was confident about his location. And Isaac also knew that every location was not forever. Isaac kept digging new wells in spite of the Philistine's resistance and because he kept digging and stayed determined to continue with his mission, he hit a well that he named, Rehoboth which means, "the Lord has made room for me." You have to learn not to take NO for an answer. Don't let people's resistance stop you, but keep on digging and if you keep on digging one day you too will dig your Rehoboth. The Lord will make room for you. Don't be stuck in your tradition; don't be stuck in one location; don't be stuck in your familiar. Move with the timing of God.

God sent Elijah, during a time of drought to the brook of Cherith. And the ravens came to the brook and brought food to Elijah day and night. But once the brook dried up, the ravens stopped coming and Elijah had to have a yielded spirit to accept the shifting of God. God was transitioning him from the brook to the widow. Because he was yielded, he received the word from God. As explained in 1 Kings 17:9 (KJV), "Arise and get thee to Zarephath. I have commanded a widow woman there to sustain thee." When you are obeying God, you cannot be stuck on your current provisions. You must be yielded to the voice of the Holy Spirit to guide you to your next place. Do not misunderstand me. I am not promoting instability, but if you are in route to a destination, it is going to take a change, movement, and sometimes relocation.

Consider the woman with the issue of blood (Mark 5:25-34) who had this issue for 12 years. I believe that her faith didn't start when she encountered Jesus. I believe she had faith before Jesus even showed up. The Bible says that she had spent money in the hands of many physicians. But, rather than her situation getting better, it grew worse. Her faith carried her from doctor to doctor; from disappointment to disappointment, all the way until her twelfth year. Even when she sees Jesus, crowds are all around Him but that still did not stop her. She said within herself, "If I could touch His garment, I will be made whole." Her faith literally became her transportation for twelve years and kept her constant in her determination to be healed. Her faith carried her through all of the doctors that failed her; it carried her through the crowds; it carried her through the issue all the way to the hem of Jesus' garment. That is why the scripture says, "Faith without works is dead." It was her faith that caused her to make contact with her answer. That is why Jesus, when He saw her, said, "Thy faith has made thee whole." The word "made" means "produced," put together by various "ingredients." Jesus didn't take the credit for her healing. He said, "Your faith has produced this success." Her ingredients were her determination to not lose hope in her healing for twelve years; to press through the crowd and make contact with her answer. So, her faith, her determination and her contact with Jesus produced her healing.

Jesus was teaching at a house in Capernaum and a man that was sick with palsy had four friends determined for him to be healed. When they got to the house, there were so many people there that they could not enter the door. But that did not stop them. They were so determined that this would be the day of their friends healing, they lifted him to the top of the house, busted a hole through the roof, and lowered this man in his bed down to Jesus.

The Bible says, "Jesus, seeing their faith..." In other words, they got Jesus' attention. They did something that nobody else did. They went above and beyond to make contact with Jesus. Sometimes you can't blend into the crowd when you need a breakthrough. You've got to go above and beyond and do something that nobody else is doing to get your breakthrough. These men were not average but their faith transported them through the crowds to the top of the house and down to Jesus, and their friend was made whole because of their faith. Jesus needs to see your unstoppable faith.

Now you must realize that when you possess faith from God, it will cause you to be determined, unstoppable, unwavering and constant. You must pursue your goals and be consistent in your mission. Be consistent in personality, consistent in character and consistent in emotions. When you have lost your determination in your pursuit, you will remain at a stand still, but if you hold these truths and keep the faith, you will keep moving and keep pressing and keep digging your way out of everything that holds you back. You must become unstoppable. Within you, God has given you the ability to continue.

> *"I press toward the mark for the prize of the high calling of God in Christ Jesus."*
> *Philippians 3:14 (KJV)*

The Indestructible You

THE INDESTRUCTIBLE YOU

Indestructible: incapable of being destroyed, ruined, or rendered ineffective.
(Merriam-Webster Dictionary)

"We are hard pressed on every side, but not crushed; perplexed, but not in despair; persecuted, but not abandoned; struck down, but not destroyed."
2 Corinthians 4:8-9 (NIV)

In 2 Corinthians, the Apostle Paul teaches that we have trouble on every side. So as believers we must anticipate unexpected problems. But verse 8 and 9 describes that the problems believers have are ineffective in their attempts to prosper. We are "hard pressed on every side" and being pressed hard is supposed to crush you. But the Bible says, but not crushed. Wow, that is awesome. "Pressed... but not crushed." The enemy's design for pressure in your life cannot crush you. "We are perplexed." Perplexities are designed to overwhelm us but even in our perplexed situations, according to the word of God, they cannot bring us to overwhelming despair. "Persecuted but not abandoned." There are times when persecutions come from all directions of your life and you feel that everybody has left and forgotten you. But the good thing about God is that we can't take other people's actions and relate them to God's. I have come to a place that when people leave you, it is a perfect time for God to take you in and take you up. So, when people come against you don't ever feel abandoned. This is my favorite part, "Struck down, but not destroyed." You have to realize that even that last hit that you took in your life was designed to destroy you, eliminate you and cause you not to exist any more. But you are so powerful that even though you got cast down, knocked down and beat down, that hit did not have enough power to destroy you. You have to realize that you will continue to exist beyond your circumstances because you are more powerful than your enemy. Let me be perfectly clear that this does not apply to everyone because you and I both know people that have been cast down and it destroyed them. They have been perplexed and could not deal with the despair and thus, took their own lives. This level right here is exclusively for believers who will put their confidence in Jesus Christ. When you are confident, you have the assurance that you will continue to exist beyond your trouble.

> *"No weapon that is formed against thee shall prosper; and every tongue that shall rise against thee in judgment thou shalt condemn. This is the heritage of the servants of the LORD, and their righteousness is of me, saith the LORD."*
> *Isaiah 54:17 (KJV)*

In the book of Jeremiah, chapter 1, when God called Jeremiah He totally equipped him to weather any storm that would come into his life.

> *"Today I have made you a fortified city, an iron pillar and a bronze wall to stand against the whole land—against the kings of Judah, its officials, its priests and the people of the land."*
> *Jeremiah 1:18 (NIV)*

Not only was Jeremiah predestined, called and anointed, he was also protected. With all that God has invested inside of us, He has to protect what He has created. God told Jeremiah, "I have made you a fortified city." A fortified city is a city that is surrounded by huge stones to keep the enemy from overtaking and conquering it. So when the enemy from an opposing kingdom would try to penetrate a city that is fortified, it was very difficult because as their men went on top of the wall the army within the city had the ability to take their enemies out without their enemies completely overtaking them. A fortified city cannot be completely overwhelmed because it is completely surrounded. I am not saying that it cannot be penetrated, but it cannot be completely consumed. So, yes, there are things that can happen to you but they cannot overtake you because the Lord has made you a fortified city.

The second thing that God made Jeremiah was an iron pillar. Iron is a metal that is unyielding and inflexible. God calls Jeremiah to have the power not to yield to his temptations or yield to the influence of others. God made Jeremiah inflexible so that he would not bend to the status quo of his time. God has made you an iron pillar. You are unyielding and inflexible.

The third thing that God made Jeremiah was a bronze wall. Bronze is a metal that is made up of two metals: copper and tin. It is also a metal that is corrosion resistant. There are going to be some places and some environments that God will allow you to enter into that have the capability of causing you to corrode and decay. But God is going to allow you to be in bad environments and not let the environment corrupt your integrity. You have the power to remain who you are in spite of your surroundings. Shadrach, Meschach and Abed-Nego were placed into a fiery furnace that was so hot that it destroyed the men that put them inside it. But they walked away without being burned or even the smell of smoke. That is what you are. You are a bronze wall. You are corrosion resistant. You are going to come out of your dilemmas without the smell of smoke. What destroyed other people cannot destroy you. Someone has died from the same thing you survived, and the reason why you survived is because when God made you, He made you with the storm in mind. You better expect to go through the flood and the fire and come out clean. A thousand shall fall at thy right hand, and ten thousand at thy left hand but nothing shall destroy you. Expect to stay alive to make it to your appointment with destiny. You are indestructible.

ABOUT THE AUTHOR

Dr. Orrin K. Pullings, Sr. is a faith-filled, prophetic pastor who has been taking the world by storm since the early age of 17. Armed with the Word of God and a heart for God's people, Dr. Orrin Pullings is the founder and Senior Pastor of United Nations Church International in Richmond, Virginia. Under his leadership he co-founded and oversees United Nations Church of New York, Georgia and South Carolina. He is the founder and overseer of United Nations Church International Assemblies.

A man of global vision and destiny, Dr. Pullings is an international conference host and speaker who has a television ministry, "Faith Charge," that reaches over 190 countries and over 80 million homes in the United States. Dr. Pullings is determined to take the gospel of the kingdom to all nations and people, while still tending to domestic needs.

Dr. Orrin K. Pullings, Sr. is a noted community leader and humanitarian whose extensive efforts garner him local and national recognition. In addition to his spiritual and civic exploits, Dr. Pullings is an accomplished scholar. He is the recipient of three academic/professional degrees from F.I. Christian University: a bachelor's degree in Biblical Studies; a master's degree in Christian Education; and a

Doctorate in Ministry. He also recently received a Doctorate of Divinity from St. Thomas Christian College.

This pastor, preacher, teacher, scholar, and life-coach is changing the lives of people by motivating them to believe God for the impossible both naturally and spiritually. The fruit of his labor is evidenced as United Nations Church International—Richmond is one the fastest growing churches in the state of Virginia. This congregation is expanding spiritually and economically, especially in the realms of entrepreneurship and education. With the release of Dr. Pullings' book, *Unstoppable Faith*, now you too have access to Dr. Pullings' life changing, faith provoking ministry—a ministry that will enable and equip you to perpetually soar to heights greater than you have ever imagined.

Dr. Pullings is the proud husband of Dr. Medina Pullings and the proud father of their four sons Orrin Jr., Elijah, James and Zacchaeus and daughter, Medina.

PUBLIC APPEARANCES

Dr. Orrin Pullings is available for:
~ Speaking Engagements ~
~ Book Signings ~
~ Workshops & Conferences ~

To request Dr. Pullings for your church,
community or organizational function,
or for prayer or consultation,
please contact him:

via e-mail:
info@unitednationschurch.org

via postal mail:
5200 Midlothian Turnpike
Richmond, VA 23225

Also, visit Dr. Pullings on the web at:
www.unitednationschurch.org

Thank you for your interest.

Perception CD/DVD $15/$20

The Treasure Series
4 CDs 31.99/4 DVD series 45.99

*Purchase these dynamic teachings
by Dr. Medina Pullings:*

Power & Authority
CD/DVD $15/$20

Suffering Establishes You
CD/DVD $15/$20

Marriage & Relationship Series

Marriage and Relationship Series
3 CD series 25.99/3 DVD series 39.99

Drs. Orrin & Medina Pullings share sound Biblical and foundational principles for building and maintaining a successful & Godly marriage & relationship.

To order additional copies of **UNSTOPPABLE FAITH:**
please forward your check or money order
(plus shipping and handling) to:

Orrin Pullings Ministries
c/o *UNSTOPPABLE FAITH*
5200 Midlothian Turnpike, Richmond, VA 23225
(e-mail) info@unitednationschurch.org
(web address) www.unitednationschurch.org

SHIPPING & HANDLING: *Please add $3.50 shipping per item ordered. For orders placed outside of the U.S., add $6.50 shipping per item.*

Qty.	Item	Unit Cost	Total
	Unstoppable Faith ___ Soft Cover 16.95 ___ Hardcover 21.95		
	Marriage and Relationship Series ___ 3 CDs 25.99 ___ 3 DVDs 39.99		
	Treasure Series ___ 4 CDs 31.99 ___ 4 DVDs 45.99		
	Perception ___ CD - $15.00 ___ DVD $20.00		
	Power & Authority ___ CD - $15.00 ___ DVD $20.00		
	Suffering Establishes You ___ CD - $15.00 ___ DVD $20.00		
		Subtotal	
		Shipping	
		Grand Total	

**Please complete shipping and billing information
on reverse side of this form.**

SHIPPING INFORMATION:

_____ _____ (Mr./Mrs./Ms.) _____
Last Name   First Name

_____
Street Address

_____, _____ _____ _____
City   State   Zip

Phone: (____)_____ E-mail:_____

BILLING INFORMATION:

_____ _____ (Mr./Mrs./Ms.) _____
Last Name   First Name

_____
Street Address

_____, _____ _____ _____
City   State   Zip

Phone: (____)_____ E-mail:_____

PAYMENT TYPE: (   ) Check   (   ) Money Order

(   ) Visa   (   ) MC   (   ) AMEX

Credit Card #:

_____

Expiration Date: _____   CVV _____
                                              (3 digits on back of card)

THANK YOU FOR PLACING YOUR ORDER

~ NOTES ~

~ NOTES ~

~ NOTES ~

~ NOTES ~

~ NOTES ~

~ NOTES ~

~ NOTES ~

~ NOTES ~

~ NOTES ~

~ NOTES ~

~ NOTES ~

~ NOTES ~

~ NOTES ~

~ **NOTES** ~

~ NOTES ~

~ NOTES ~